Person-C
Prayer Ministry

John Leach

Acting Rector, St Lawrence, Jersey

GROVE BOOKS LIMITED

RIDLEY HALL RD CAMBRIDGE CB3 9HU

Contents

1	Person-Centred Prayer Ministry	3
2	Why Another Model?	5
3	Explaining the Model	9
4	Person-Centred Prayer Ministry in Action	17
5	Using Person-Centred Prayer Ministry	22
6	Just Do It!	28
	Notes	28

Acknowledgments

Grateful thanks are due to all those who have attended ARM *Developing Prayer Ministry* Training Days and who have helped hone this material for publication. Special thanks too go to Roger Harper for his friendship and his help in the writing of this book, and to David Newman for its title.

The Cover Illustration is by Peter Ashton

First Impression October 2003
ISSN 1470-8531
ISBN 1 85174 544 0

Person-Centred Prayer Ministry 1

The creature's foetid breath brushed my cheek as she moved in closer, an evil light shining from her eyes.

Terrified, I held my breath as a clawed hand came towards my face, and then gripped my temples, almost drawing blood. At the same instant I felt another hand grasp my shoulder and begin to force me to the ground. A cold shiver ran down my spine as I watched the evil jaws open, just by a small crack, so that I could see the yellow fangs and the drool running down her chin. In a sepulchral voice like something from a far distant world, the creature began to speak. Waves of panic hit me as the fateful sounds were uttered from between thin blue and black lips, 'You need to forgive your mother-in-law!'

'If I do ever manage to get out of here alive and intact,' I vowed to myself, 'I will never again respond to a word of knowledge!'

Prayer ministry can be like that, can't it? When it is good it is very very good, but when it is bad it is rotten. My background is that of a convinced Wimberite, and for nineteen years I have found the Vineyard model for prayer ministry the most helpful, accessible and powerful. But when I met up with Ian Wood and Margaret Waight from Renewal Ministries in New Zealand (a kind of Presbyterian equivalent of Anglican Renewal Ministries, for whom I used to work), and they mentioned that God had led them into a new model for prayer ministry which minimized some of the dangers of current models, I had to know more. It was from my encounter with them that what I call 'Person-Centred Prayer Ministry' evolved. The aim of the book is to introduce the model, and explain a bit about *why* it is useful, and *where* it might be useful. A quick note on terminology might be in order here. I shall use the terms 'pray-er' and 'minister' interchangeably to describe the person or persons 'doing' the prayer ministry, although, as we will soon see, in the person-centred model the very concept of someone 'doing it' is less than helpful. Clearly in using the word 'minister' I am using shorthand for 'prayer minister,' and not saying anything at all about restricting prayer to the ordained or those in church

When it is good it is very very good, but when it is bad it is rotten

leadership. But in describing the person to whom it is done, the person coming with a need to receive ministry, we have a more complicated task. I will follow in this book my usual convention of rejecting the terms 'patient' as too medical, 'client' as too professional, 'person being prayed for' as too lengthy, and 'prayee' as too silly. Instead I will use the term 'victim' because it gets a cheap laugh when I am speaking and is in a real sense theologically accurate.

The person-centred model can be useful in a much wider range of situations

And so to prayer ministry. Let me make two points right from the start. Firstly, there is much in the person-centred model which is not new—some of the ways of praying which it uses will seem rather old-hat to seasoned pray-ers. I claim no novelty for it, but I do think that the methods it uses have often been restricted too much in their application, particularly to the realms of what has come to be called 'Inner Healing' or 'Healing of the Memories.' The person-centred model can be useful in a much wider range of situations.

Secondly, it is important to understand that I am not trying to sell you the person-centred model as a panacea which makes any other ways of ministering redundant. Rather, I want to suggest that it might prove to be a useful tool to keep in one's kit alongside other ways of praying, rather than instead of them.

Negative Experiences of Prayer Ministry

'He pushed me over!'

'She had a "prophecy" for me which was completely unhelpful and irrelevant.'

'They prayed about what they thought I needed, not what I wanted.'

'When I didn't get up and walk they told me it was my fault.'

'I felt manipulated.'

'Nobody bothered to listen.'

'They started trying to cast out the spirit of a broken leg.'

'At the end I felt I had been somehow violated.'

Why Another Model? 2

Let me say again that I am a great fan of the Vineyard model of prayer ministry.

I have used it for 19 years, taught it to literally thousands of people, and shall continue to do so into the future. However, I have come to realize that when handled less than perfectly it can lead to some unhelpful dynamics, and may not be the most helpful model in some situations. I often ask people to share their negative experiences of prayer ministry; some of the responses I have received are the facing page. I think it is possible to group these problems under four general headings.

1 Power and Dependency

The traditional 'pentecostal' model of prayer ministry, against which John Wimber quite understandably reacted, was that anyone responding to a call for ministry (usually for healing, salvation or Baptism in the Spirit) would come forward and receive passively while the gifted 'healer' did it 'to them.' The emphasis of Wimber and others on giving the ministry back to the body of Christ and not just the superstar at the front is surely to be welcomed,[1] but there can still be an element of being 'done to.'

The victim is encouraged not to pray or join in, but to switch off and just receive; God may speak during the encounter with prophetic or revelatory words or pictures, but usually through the pray-er. The person-centred model changes these power dynamics by involving the victims and letting them lead the process.

The person-centred model changes these power dynamics by involving the victims

I often ask people when I am teaching to compare and contrast the different ways in which they would be treated should they need the ministrations of a surgeon and/or a midwife. Surgeons would work intrusively and invasively with the patient completely anaesthetized; they would be doing something unnatural because something had gone wrong with the patients; they would be treating their patients merely as bodies to be cut into; and so on. A midwife, on the other hand, would simply be there to coach and to co-operate with a natural process in which the mother would be consciously doing all the hard work. Now I am not implying that a midwife is in any way *better* than a surgeon; if I get appendicitis do *not* bring me a midwife! But I am simply illustrating that in person-centred prayer ministry the role of the prayer is much more akin to that of a midwife than a surgeon. And since the victim is much more active, it can lessen the tendency for an individual to keep coming back again and again for ministry because he or she thrives on the attention and thus moves towards dependency.

The role of the pray er is much more ak to that of a midwife than a surgeon

2 Inaccuracy

The Vineyard model is very hot on listening to God; it is often driven by words of knowledge, it seeks ongoing revelation from the Spirit during the process, and may major on prophetic input into people's lives. I have no quibble with this at all, as long as it is accurate. But inevitably from time to time we will get it wrong. It may be that we mishear God, for a variety of reasons which may be nothing more than that we are just a bit overtired. There need be nothing sinister here—just the weakness of the flesh or our inexperience. Experience, on the other hand, can also militate against accurate hearing of God; our pastoral skills and our natural knowledge of the victim, or of others in similar situations whom we have encountered, may tempt us strongly to tell our victims what we think would be good for them. This can mean that a prayer session degenerates into nothing more than good advice or amateur counselling. This can be particularly manipulative if our advice is couched in terms which help the victim to think that it is prophetic or in some way 'God's word for me' when it may be nothing more than a helpful hint or, at worst, an expression of our own frustration with the victim. Many of those I have spoken to report being hurt by inaccurate or ill-advised 'prophetic' input into their lives during sessions of ministry. Person-centred prayer ministry, like its namesake counselling method, refuses to put onto people our own agendas for them, and encourages them hear from the Spirit directly.

Many of those I have spoken to report being hurt by inaccurate or ill-advised 'prophetic' input into their lives

3 Verbosity

Again, the Vineyard model quite rightly reacts against some of the wordy evangelical praying captured so beautifully by Peter Lawrence:

> O Lord, we do just lift up sister Ellen's left leg to you, just as we lifted up her right leg to you last week. We do just thank you, Lord, that Ellen has been arranging the flowers in our church so beautifully for thirty-five years and has never missed a jumble sale. And Lord, we do thank you that as I preached last week with a good introduction, three clear points and a conclusion, you always listen to us and do whatever we tell you. And so, Lord, before this congregation and before the host of heaven and before the football scores come on the television, I ask you to come in power and might and heal this leg. Amen.[2]

However, it is fundamentally a word-based model; if the minister does receive a 'picture' for the victim, it still has to be described to them in words for them to be able to access it. Person-centred prayer ministry is far more image-based, which, while it may make it more difficult for some who work exclusively with words, allows greater accessibility to those less at home with the linear, logical and verbal. Children, for example, or those with various learning difficulties, ought to find it a more helpful model.

It allows greater accessibility to those less at home with the linear, logical and verbal

4 Accessibility

But the greatest problem with the Vineyard model, particularly among those with whom I usually work, is its highly all-or-nothing nature. To accept ministry can put a person in a very vulnerable position. You may have to get up and go to the front, receive prayer in public, perhaps with hundreds of people watching. You may possibly find yourself exhibiting various forms of behaviour under the unction of the Spirit such as laughing, crying, shaking, jerking or falling over. On one level I have no problem with this. As a vicar I was often asked if prayer ministry could be a little more private, and my stock answer was to point to Bartimaeus in Mark 10 and tell people that those who received what they wanted from Jesus tended to be those who were desperate enough to admit their need, and not to care who knew about it. While this may have been God's word for my somewhat proud and privatized parish, I have since changed my mind a bit.

In my itinerant ministry I have discovered that there is a lot more prayer ministry talked about than actually done in renewed churches. I have lost count of the number of times people have told me that they do have a ministry team and they do offer prayer after services but 'no-one ever comes forward.' The problem may well lie in the model we use; it can be a bit too dangerous for your average struggling-painfully-towards-renewal church.

This is often compounded by the fact that it is not seen as a part of our worship; if there is to be ministry we do it after the service has ended as a slightly more spiritual alternative to coffee, so that those who are into that kind of thing can take part while the rest scuttle for the safety of the urn and the polystyrene cups. Person-centred prayer ministry can be used in ways which make it accessible and non-threatening to people, and may open the doors to the possibility of other types of ministry at a later stage. I often say that in my quest for a model I want one I could use at my 8 o'clock Communion service. This one I can!

If there is to be ministry we do it after the service has ended as a slightly more spiritual alternative to coffee

Of course much current prayer ministry is indeed accurate, Spirit-led, and ultimately helpful, but few of us will have escaped entirely from the more negative aspects which can be a part of it. The person-centred model does not guarantee perfect ministry every time—prayer ministers can mess up most models if they try hard enough—but if done properly it does make unhelpful practices less likely. And, as we shall see, its applications are very widespread, from corporate ministry times in large gatherings, to one-to-one ministry, with non-Christians on aeroplanes, and even during sacramental confession. It is every bit as Spirit-guided as more familiar models, but it allows for the Spirit to speak directly to the victim without always going through the channel of the minister.

Explaining the Model

3

It was the genius of John Wimber that he was able to condense healing ministry into five simple steps; the wide popularity of his model must be partly due to the way it was made so easily accessible.

I have managed to get the person-centred model down to nine steps, which is nearly as easy, but like the Vineyard model it is much more free-flowing in practice than the useful teaching aid would suggest. I will set out the stages first, then discuss each of them, and end with some examples of the model in practice.

Person-centred Prayer Ministry—the Process

1 Identify the issue
2 Identify an image—significance?
3 Identify location—significance?
4 Invite the Holy Spirit
5 The victim prays
6 The minister prays
7 Waiting
8 Feedback
9 Closure and blessing, *or* back to stage 2

So what does all that mean? Let us look at each stage in turn.

1 Identify the Issue

For what is the person seeking prayer? What is it that has caused him to seek it? Response to the preaching of the Word? A specific word of knowledge? A touch of the Spirit during worship? A situation which he has brought along with him? There might be a whole variety of different agendas, sparked off by many different things. Those experienced in prayer ministry will know that only a small proportion of needs presented for prayer are to do with physical healing. Some would say that the increased stress of modern living, coupled with the relative accessibility of effective medical care, has shifted the balance of needs found in the biblical healing stories away from the physical and towards the emotional and relational. Whether or not this is true, it is certainly the case that a whole variety of needs may be presented for ministry.

It is worth mentioning as well that person-centred prayer ministry need not be exclusively negative; it can be used to give thanks in good times as well as to pray for help in bad times.

The minister listens carefully to the victim at this stage, and helps hin or her articulate a need or an issue specific enough to get hold of in prayer.

2 Identify an Image

The minister then asks the victim to identify an image of God which they feel would be an appropriate one in this situation. This question may be framed as 'How would you like God to come to you right now?' 'What do you need God to be for you at the moment?' or even by asking them to complete the sentence 'Right now I need God to come and be my…' What is needed is a specific and concrete image.

The image may come from three different sources, or a combination of them. Firstly it may be a specific image or even a title of God used in Scripture. 'I need God to come to me as my shepherd,' 'my healer,' 'my guide,' and so on, would be useful responses.

Secondly, the image may come not directly from the Bible but from the created world; 'I need God to come to me as a rushing river,' 'a cool refreshing pool,' 'a cave of shelter,' 'my rock.' There may be some overlap with the Bible, of course, even if the image is not a specific biblical title for God.

What is needed is a specific and concrete image

Thirdly, the image may be from the contemporary world, and may have very little at all apparently to do with the Bible. This is fine, as long as the image is one which is compatible with the character of God as revealed in Scripture. Although I could not find it anywhere in my concordance, I felt it fine to go along with someone who said they needed God to be their dustbin.

The real point of this stage in the process, though, is the supplementary question, once the image has been identified, 'What would be the significance of that for you?' The biblical image of 'shepherd,' for example, has many nuances—feeding, caring, nurturing, leading, protecting, to name but a few. So the first question above is followed with this one, which has the function of helping the victim to clarify exactly what he would like God to be or do for him.

This question is particularly important when a contemporary image is selected; on one occasion someone said they wanted God to come to them like Arnie Schwarzenegger in *Terminator*. Was that consistent with the character of God as revealed in Scripture? At first sight the answer seemed to be a resounding 'No'! The supplementary 'What would be the significance of that for you?' however, indicated that it was indeed, as the significance was said to be that he would never stop, would never be prevented by any barrier from doing what he purposed to do (and, as a pedantic eschatological theologian who was present pointed out, 'He'll be back!'). Sometimes we need to swallow our instantaneous reactions and our desire, in the name of orthodoxy, to put people right, and just learn to listen a bit longer and a bit more carefully.

> *Sometimes we need to swallow our instantaneous reactions and our desire to put people right*

3 Identify a Location

The next question is 'Where would you like God to be placed in relation to you?' Answers might include 'In front of me to lead me,' 'With me nestled on his lap,' 'Beside me with his arm around me' and so on. Again this is followed by the supplementary 'What would be the significance of that?' which might get answers like 'I cannot see where to go, so I need him to show me the way' or 'I am feeling so unloved by other people at the moment that I need God to show his love by a cuddle.' The point of this stage is to help the victim to see a clear mental picture rather than thinking theological concepts The question of position or location can help to sharpen up this image and make it easier to 'see.'

Some people may of course find it difficult initially to think in pictorial terms. The minister may need to help them sharpen up the image away from a vague or theoretical answer ('I need God to forgive me') towards a more concrete image (I need God to come as a High-court judge to bang his little mallet and say to me 'Case dismissed!'). Theologically over-scrupulous ministers may find some images difficult, and may occasionally not find the 'significance' question helps, so that some gentle steering towards a more biblical image is achieved. 'I need God to come with a machine-gun to kill all my teachers' could be tempered slightly by acknowledging the very real anger the victim is feeling, but then asking what she thinks Jesus did to those who were out to get him and murder him. 'What do you think God might want to do to your teachers really?' could provoke a better answer, whilst not diminishing in any way the unsanctified but very natural feelings of the victim, nor making her feel too guilty for experiencing them.

An important question presents itself here: from where do the images come? Is it that the victim thinks up something which might fit the bill, or dredges around their scant knowledge of the Bible in order to come up with an image which will satisfy the minister? The only answer I can give from my experience of using this model is that the image comes from the Holy Spirit. The passage in Romans 8 about the Spirit helping us when we do not know how to pray comes to mind. I am sure this interpretation does not exhaust the meaning of the verse, but it does seem to be an example of it in action. People say, significantly often, something like 'I don't know where that picture came from' or 'I just heard myself saying that when you asked.' It is also not uncommon for those who are familiar with the model, and who are thus expecting the question, to have a thought-out answer prepared, only to find an entirely different image appearing to them, even as they begin to speak. Neither is it uncommon to find that the image changes as the ministry unfolds. I can only conclude that the Spirit of God is active in this process, knowing as he does our own needs and the mind of the Father so much more clearly than we do.

It is not uncommon to find that the image changes as the ministry unfolds

4 Invite the Holy Spirit

One of the key elements of the 'Wimber' model was the inviting (or 'epiclesis') of the Holy Spirit to be present and to guide the encounter, and this is every bit as important here. The minister (or indeed the victim) can say a simple prayer of welcome to the Spirit, which has more to do with acknowledging his presence than summoning an otherwise absent deity. The rest of the ministry session is placed under his control and guidance. Jesus reminded us that no father would give something harmful when we ask for something good; how much more willingly does our heavenly Father give us the Holy Spirit when we ask him.

5 The Victim Prays

Here is the key distinctive of the person-centred model: the minister asks the victim to form a short prayer asking God to come as whatever and wherever he has decided he needs in the earlier stages, which the victim then prays out loud. Something along the lines of 'Dear God, please come to me as a rock to protect me. Let me hide behind you from those who are trying to harm me' is all that is needed. Some victims have never prayed out loud before; they may not even be active Christians. A simple prayer prayed by the pray-er a phrase at a time, and repeated out loud will usually do the trick, and may even have the effect of breaking the sound-barrier for the person, so that he or she can begin to feel confident in vocal prayer in other settings. With the statistics reminding us that the vast majority of people in Britain pray, even though very few would attend or associate themselves with church, the need for someone to do their own praying when they may not yet have a Christian commitment usually presents no problem.

What is vitally important here, though, is that if a prayer is framed for them it represents accurately what they have said in answer to the earlier questions, and is not in any way interpretative on the part of the minister.

6 The Minister Prays

This principle is vital at this stage too, as the minister adds her own prayer to that of the victim, *but only ever using* the victim's *images, words and pictures*. The prayer should be no longer than that of the victim, and should contain no extra interpretative material, different pictures, even if given to you by God, no personal slant on what their problems are *really* about, and no horizontal prayers which are thinly-disguised attempts to give good advice ('Dear Lord, strengthen her to cut down from 60-a-day so that her health will get better'). Counsellors trained in the Rogerian or client-centred therapeutic model will be familiar with the technique of 'reflecting back,' and will also know how notoriously difficult it is in the early stages of learning. This is reflecting back in prayer, and can be just as difficult until with practice it becomes second nature.

The prayer should be no longer than that of the victim, and should contain no extra interpretative material

The minister's prayer for the victim may at this stage be accompanied by the laying-on-of hands, if that feels appropriate to both people. If in doubt, ask: 'How would you feel if I just put a hand on your shoulder as we pray? Would you be comfortable with that?' The power of touch can be very healing in itself, even without us needing to think in terms of power flowing, electric currents and the like, which again reinforce the sometimes unhelpful sense that if God is going to do anything he is going to do it *through* me.

7 Waiting

Then follows a period of silence and waiting, in which the victim is engaged with God and the minister waits, praying silently, perhaps in tongues. There may or may not be physical manifestations visible to the minister, but what is typically going on is that the victim is watching a Spirit-given video playing in his head as he visualizes the coming of God to him according to his image. The minister should be with the victim, both physically and in spirit, during this waiting time, but should do nothing which might distract or interrupt it, for example violent hand-shaking or muttering semi-audibly in tongues. When it feels right (and there is no set way of knowing when that is, so it is a matter of 'feel'), the minister moves gently on to the next phase.

8 Feedback

A question such as 'Is anything happening for you?' will allow victims to reflect on their experience of the last few minutes. In telling the story of what they have seen or experienced, things may clarify in their own minds. The minister should avoid asking 'What was going on for you?' since this implies that something should have been. 'Is anything…?' allows the possibility that they experienced nothing at all. However, very rarely, in my experience, will people say that nothing at all has been going on; more typically they will have 'seen' God dealing with them in some way. What happens is usually based around their image, at least to begin with, although the Spirit may then take them off in some other, unexpected direction. Again, the job of the minister is not to interpret or advise, but simply to listen attentively and let the story be told.

The job of the minister is not to interpret or advise, but simply to let the story be told

There may be, at this point or sometimes earlier, emotional release through tears or joy (or both!). As with other models, ministers should not allow human sympathy to take over and swamp their victim with hugs and shallow reassurance. We need to learn the art of standing back and letting the Spirit do his work.

9 Closure and Blessing, or Back to Stage 2

At this point, a decision has to be made. Sometimes the experience of the victim under the power of the Spirit will feel as if it has led to what I think is most helpfully called 'closure.' That does not mean that all the problems the victim will ever have are dealt with once and for all, but it does mean that the work for this session is finished, that the Spirit has led them to a positive and clear point where they can safely and happily be left. If that is the case, the minister may close the encounter with a simple prayer for God's blessing, that he will keep the image before the victim in the days ahead, and that he will bring to fruition the work he has been doing. If the minister has received any words or pictures from God for the victim at any point during the process, they may be shared at this point. Of course they should be shared carefully and as suggestions rather than as 'Thus saith the Lord…' statements from which there is no escape! However, in my experience this is often superfluous, since the things I have sensed God saying to me were communicated exactly to the victim whilst they were engaged with God. In that case I may tell them 'That was exactly what *I* felt God was saying too,' which makes them feel good because what they were hearing was confirmed by me, rather than making me look good because I am the one to whom God speaks. This is another example of the way in which this model empowers rather than reinforcing dependency.

This is another example of the way in which this model empowers rather than reinforcing dependency

Sometimes, however, closure will not have been reached at this point, and there may be more work to do. This story illustrates:

Jim had been feeling stressed and overworked, and decided that he needed God to come like a flowing river to refresh him. He prayed, the minister prayed, and then he was able to visualize himself swimming and floating in cool water. But then things moved on, and the Spirit showed him a picture of himself climbing out of the water, only to be besieged by many people clamouring for his attention. This was clearly not closure, since things were worse than when the exercise began. So the minister decided to return to stage 2 and begin again: 'You feel besieged by the demands of other people: how do you need God to come to you now?' This time the image which came immediately and unexpectedly to mind was that of a large tea-strainer (another good biblical term for God).

'What would be the significance of that?' asked the minister.

'I want God to allow only those people whom he wants me to spend time with to get to me, and I want him to filter out all those whom it is not my task to deal with.' So the process went round again, with a simple prayer for God to come to Jim like a tea-strainer, a period of waiting, and some feedback. Jim saw people being filtered out, and was even able to identify some particular individuals who had been adding to his stress, whom he now understood God to be saying were not his concern. Final closure was reached, and Jim was able to go away and take specific action to make his life less stressful. Refreshing in the river was only a temporary answer; the prayer now was for a more radical reprioritization.

In theory the process could go round and round for ever, but I would think that the point would come when more persistent problems, or a victim who was unable at all to think positively and receive what God was doing, would suggest a need for deeper and more professional counselling and ministry. As with other models of ministry, the most important thing to know is what you do not know and when to call in someone who knows more than you do.

Person-Centred Prayer Ministry in Action

4

That is the theory, then. But what does it look like in real life?

To illustrate the theory better, here are a couple of accounts of real ministry sessions. They are of course used with permission, and names and a few details have been changed to preserve confidentiality.

Peter is an ordained Baptist minister who has an itinerant ministry rather than running a single church. He went to a conference feeling worn out with the constant travelling, and in need of a new vision for his work. He had also been experiencing some rejection as traditionalist people responded negatively to the message he was bringing, that the denomination needed to change radically if it was to survive and be a force for the kingdom into the future.

During a ministry time he was invited to consider what he needed God to be for him, and before he had time to think the word 'raven' popped into his mind. He did not realize its significance at that stage, but it was such a strong impression that he went with it anyway, and invited God to come to him as a raven. Immediately he saw himself as the prophet Elijah taking a break from his public ministry and resting by the brook while God provided for him. As the ministry time continued he became aware of God's desire to nourish him, not as a permanent escape from his calling but as a temporary refreshment. Soon the picture changed and he saw himself standing on a rock preaching to the people with new vigour and vision.

Peter is now refreshed and back in ministry, but he says that the image of God as the raven is one which returns to him again and again, particularly during times of stress, and gives him permission to rest and enjoy God's care for him.

Mary was in her early 60s. She had cervical spondilitis from an accident on her factory shop-floor nine years earlier. She had to stop work, and was given high padded collars for her painful neck. Her arms and hands were affected as well as her neck. She wore her collar when the pain became too bad.

In a healing service at church a visiting speaker had a word of knowledge which Mary thought was for her, so she went forward for prayer. She was asked if she forgave the company for her injury, to which she replied brightly 'Oh yes!' She then received prayer and laying-on-of-hands. Back in her seat afterwards she noticed to her delight that her hands were less swollen; they have remained better ever since.

Mary's neck was still painful at times though, and she would sometimes ask for prayer from the church's prayer ministry team. One member particularly would stand behind her with his hands on her head and neck. She would feel warmth coming to her neck and the pain would ease, although after a little while it would return.

Then one day Mary asked the vicar to go and see her to talk about a Thanksgiving service for her son's new baby. Before he left he asked her how she was and she said that her neck was bad again. The vicar decided to try using a different method of ministry, and asked her how and where she needed God to come to her. After a little while she settled on Jesus coming as her healer, standing behind her and putting his hands on her head and neck, just as the member of the ministry team used to.

The vicar invited the Holy Spirit to come to Mary and himself. Then Mary and the vicar asked Jesus to come as her healer, and to stand behind her. Mary was sitting on her settee in the centre of her small council house living room, and the vicar could see that she seemed to be focusing on something but did not know what. After a time of quiet, with the vicar praying quietly, he asked her if anything was happening.

Jesus was not standing behind he but in front of her

Mary said that she had not understood it at first. Jesus was not standing behind her but in front of her. He was not putting his hands on her head or neck. She thought he was in the wrong place! The vicar encouraged her to accept this and thanked Jesus for coming to her, inviting him to keep coming to her.

Mary saw Jesus standing tall in front of her, a lovely man in a dullish dark red robe. He looked regal. He just stood in front of Mary and held our his hands towards her. She felt a strong warmth on her head and neck and down her back.

Before the vicar left, they thanked Jesus for his presence, and Mary said she felt much better.

Late that night Mary looked for her collar just in case she needed it nearby. She searched in her bedroom drawers where she thought it was but could not find it. Then she sensed that someone was standing in her bedroom corner saying 'O ye of little faith.' She gasped and immediately stopped looking for her collar.

Mary has not needed her collar since. Her neck has been fine. She did come across the collar recently in the place where she always thought it was, and does not quite see why she could not find it that night.

Steve was a dock-worker from Merseyside who had no church background but who had been so emotionally touched at the birth of their first baby that he and his partner approached the local church about 'christening.' However, since the birth things had not been going well in the family, and the increased stress had caused quite a bit of tension between him and Jo, to the point where he feared they might separate. The church, seeking to care for them and draw them in, had invited them to an evening service with a visiting preacher.

Jo was at home looking after the baby, but Steve came, and sat alone at the back. He survived the sermon with little comprehension, but at the end of the talk the preacher invited the congregation to close their eyes and imagine how they wanted God to come to them in their different needs. He prayed a bit more, and the service ended. As people left the church the speaker noticed a big muscular crew-cut man sitting in his seat sobbing. He went over and asked if the man wanted to talk. Steve told him that when he had been asked to imagine how he wanted God to come he had asked Jesus to come and put his arms round the family to hold them together. Suddenly he opened his eyes and looked around; he had felt physically a hand wrap round his shoulders. He thought it was another member of the congregation, but there was no-one at all within about five seats around him. He realized he had felt a physical touch from God, and began to cry with the sheer wonder that the Almighty God should bother to answer his prayer and come to him. He had moved one large step closer to a saving faith in Jesus.

Dave came to a workshop on healing prayer in his church in the Midlands. He was not long out of prison, and had been experiencing bad pains in his back and stomach. Three different doctors had told him three different things about what was causing the pain, from irritable bowel syndrome to a crumbling disc.

Dave wanted God to come as a rainbow. His main need was to know in what direction to go to find healing, given the conflicting things that he was being told.

The person ministering to Dave invited the Holy Spirit and they both then asked God to come as a rainbow. Dave stayed quiet for a while and was then asked if anything was going on. He said he felt peaceful. The minister thanked God for coming with peace and asked him to keep coming to Dave. They waited a little while more, and then he said again that he felt really peaceful and enjoyed the peace. The minister wondered whether to round things off then, but others were still praying and he wanted a bit more than just 'peace.' A rainbow would have been nice!

Dave relaxed again and the minister invited God to come closer, to bring more of himself. Dave looked peaceful and relaxed but then started shifting around a little in his seat. When asked after a little what was happening he said that it felt as though someone was manipulating his back from the inside. This carried on for a while and then stopped. They thanked God for what he had been doing, and Dave said that the pain in his leg which he had had earlier had gone. Dave's back continues to be significantly better, although he has had plenty of other problems to contend with.

Denise had for several months been suffering from wheezing and coughing associated with asthma. This was especially bad during the damp winter months, and she had largely accepted it, although it did seem to be getting more severe and lasting longer than usual. When it got to the point that she was rattling each time she breathed in and out she decided to go to the doctor. He advised her to increase the use of an inhaler for a month but the condition did not get any better. He then decided to put her on a course of steroids, again with negative results. On the next visit she saw a different doctor who told her that one of the tablets she was taking for high blood pressure affects asthma and that she would have to change them. Then on her last day at work before going on holiday the cough was about the worst it had been and she was extremely tired and fed up with it all, as well as getting headaches from the continuous coughing. Her vicar offered to pray for her, and she asked the Holy Spirit to come to her as a mist to encircle her and heal her of the coughing, wheezing and rattling. They waited and almost immediately there was a sense of the Holy Spirit as a mist, at first swirling around in a very gentle way. Then she was aware of inhaling this mist; as it entered her lungs it turned into a hand with a white cotton glove on it and began a circular movement within her chest. She began to feel a very warm sensation as the hand moved round. Denise was clear that this was not a picture in front of her but a definite feeling of something happening inside her. It was as though she was undergoing an operation of some kind, yet she was awake while it was being done.

Previously Denise had been a bit cynical about others' stories of encounters with Jesus, thinking that they had perhaps dressed things up a bit. But after this she was convinced. 'I know that I couldn't have imagined a mist turning into a gloved hand, and also I did not have time to think about it because it was very impromptu. What I felt was most real and what happened next is proof that it was.'

As the gloved hand continued to move, the tightness and rawness in her chest suddenly and instantly disappeared and the cough, along with the wheezing and rattling, completely vanished. At her next visit to the doctor Denise was told that there was very little to hear on her chest.

She knows that God has not completely cured her asthma but what she had wanted was an end to the persistent cough and all that came with it. This God gave her in a most profound way.

---

5 Using Person-Centred Prayer Ministry

I hope these stories give a clearer idea of the process of person-centred prayer ministry, and I want to finish by looking at three contexts in which it provides a helpful model, and how it might be adapted for use in each.

1 One-to-One

The nine-stage process as I have outlined it above is first and foremost useful in settings where an individual is ministered to by another individual in a private setting, for example at a specific pastoral appointment or in a corner somewhere after a church service. Of course I take seriously the safeguards often insisted upon that there should be more than one person doing ministry, and I agree that it is wise for 'one-to-one' to read 'two-to-one.' However, unlike other models of prayer ministry, there should be one person who is actually 'doing it,' while the other is there purely for silent prayer back-up, and possibly for feedback to the minister afterwards. It can be highly confusing for the victim, being coached and guided through the process, to be getting instruction from more than one voice. I would imagine that the only thing worse than being dealt with by a midwife would be to be dealt with by two midwives! So make it clear who is there to lead the ministry, and who is there to support and pray in the background. The process can then be worked through by the minister, and if the other person has any words or insights they may be offered sensitively during the final 'Blessing' stage.

It can be highly confusing for the victim to be getting instruction from more than one voice

2 Small Groups

The same principle applies when using this model in group settings such as homegroups; decide who is actually doing it and let the rest pray silently in the background. We were taught by John Wimber that when praying in small groups the 'anointing' might move around to different members of the group as the ministry moves through different phases, or that different pray-ers might receive some kind of revelation which could progress the ministry. But with person-centred prayer ministry this could get highly confusing for the victim, so it is best if someone is 'in charge' and that the others keep silent until the process is over, at which point 'words' or pictures may be sensitively offered.

It is best if someone is 'in charge' and that the others keep silent until the process is over

3 Church Services

But what about using person-centred prayer ministry during public worship? A couple of the stories above seemed to imply that it could work more corporately; how exactly does this happen?

In my *Developing Prayer Ministry*[3] I told the story of my Wednesday morning Communion Service where I first introduced prayer ministry to a highly traditional congregation by going half-way (or more) to meet them in terms of the model we used. If only I had known then what I know now! I have used person-centred prayer ministry in all sorts of situations, including some where no prayer ministry has ever before been offered, and I have found anything up to half the congregation responding. I suggest that this is because person-centred prayer ministry provides an accessible model when used in services, and a relatively non-threatening way of involving people in ministry. So how do I do it?

First of all, I am preaching towards a response. I explain this in more detail in my *Responding to Preaching*,[4] but fundamentally I believe that preaching ought to call forth some kind of response from people's wills, rather than merely informing their minds or occasionally touching their emotions. So when I get up to preach I know what I am going for. I try to make sure as well that there are a variety of possible responses; I know that different people can hear the same sermon saying vastly differing things to them.

So when I get up to preach I know what I am going for

At the end of the sermon I invite people to close their eyes for what I call 'a short meditation.' Then I work through the nine-stage process, but with the following variations.

1 Identify the Issue
I set out a variety of possible options which I think may have come out of the talk for people, always adding the possibility that it might not be any of those things which have touched them, but something completely unrelated but which is nevertheless on their hearts at the moment. So for example:

> Some of us might be feeling like the crowd in that story: worn out, and in need of refreshment. Some of us might feel like the little boy: we feel that our small contribution is totally inadequate to meet people's needs. Perhaps you identify with the disciples: you feel called to a task by Jesus but you just don't know how you're going to achieve it. You might even feel like a loaf of bread—you feel you've been broken in pieces in trying to feed and help others. Or maybe it's none of these things, but you just feel in need of a new touch from God, perhaps for healing, for yourself or someone close to you who's on your heart.

I am trying to be as inclusive as possible; the main aim is to help people encounter God, but the subtext is to make the whole exercise as accessible as possible for the many people who have in the past been scared off by prayer ministry or who have never felt the courage to respond.

2 Identify an Image—Significance?
Having helped people in a non-threatening way to identify a need in their lives, I would then ask them to identify how they needed God to come to them, explaining very briefly about names or images of God. I would then ask them to ask themselves silently what the significance of their choice is—why *that* image?

3 Identify Location—Significance?
After a brief pause I ask people to identify where in their mental picture they would like God to be, and again why there? What is the significance of that?

4 Invite the Holy Spirit **and**

5 The Victim Prays
I use a brief prayer of invitation to the Holy Spirit, and then invite the congregation to pray silently that God would come to them as the image they have identified. I often feed them a template prayer: 'Lord, right now I need you to come to me as…(whichever image), and to be…(wherever).'

6 The Minister Prays
I then say a short cover-all prayer along the lines of 'Lord, I want to add my prayers to the prayers of your people, that you would come to each of us in the way we most need you right now. Amen.'

7 Waiting
I would allow a brief time of silence, perhaps one minute or so, and I would be praying silently for the congregation and watching for what looks like responses to the Spirit, whether in terms of physical manifestations or emotional expressions such as tears.

8 Feedback
After a while I tell people that some of them may have felt or sensed God meeting with them or interacting in some way, perhaps in terms of 'watching a video play in your mind's eye.' I would then invite any who sensed God working with them, and would like him to intensify the image they have had, or continue something he has started, to avail themselves of the opportunity for further one-to-one ministry at some later point. I would then use a prayer of thanksgiving, and move on to the Creed or whatever.

Follow-up Ministry

Again, there are further details about handling response in *Responding to Preaching*, so I will not repeat them here, but there are a couple of guidelines which do need spelling out clearly. I have found this approach to be most helpful if the invitation for further ministry is made as easy for people as possible, and I have found over a period of time that two practices work well.

I also tell them that when they go for anointing they will receive a simple liturgical prayer

The first is that I invite people to receive anointing with oil. I am aware that in the Catholic tradition this is a solemn rite which is reserved for serious, usually terminal, illness, but anointing seems to be something which is more culturally acceptable to many nowadays, particularly those within my own Anglican tradition. I tell people that if they want to receive prayer they should go to a particular place—this of course will depend on the physical layout of the buildin—at a particular time. This will depend on the ongoing liturgy of the service. I have found that after receiving bread and wine is a good time, as people are already on their feet and can visit an anointing station on their way back to their seats.

But I also tell them, and this seems to be vitally important, that when they go for anointing they will receive a simple liturgical prayer,[5] which will be the same, or more or less the same, for everyone, and they will not be asked why they are asking for prayer, or even for whom they are seeking it. They will simply receive anointing, and then make their way back to their seats.

While those responding do not seem to have too much of a problem with this, I have found it necessary to watch those ministering, particularly if they have been trained and have been involved for any length of time in other models of ministry. If I tell people that they will receive a simple liturgical prayer, and then they go forward and get Wimber's five stages, they might with some justification feel that we have broken faith with them, and we may have taken several steps backwards in the journey towards them feeling comfortable with prayer ministry. Experienced pray-ers may feel that doing it this way is not 'real' prayer ministry, and so do their own thing anyway, but it is vital to stop this practice and insist that they do what the preacher has told the congregation they will do. There can be a kind of élitist, unsubmissive spirit among some prayer ministers, and of course it is a well-known fact that the fiercest opponents of any move of God in the church can be the children of the previous move of God! Some teaching and even confrontation may be necessary if we are to convince our prayer ministers that this model does have real value, and that they should do it your way in this kind of a context.

Experienced pray-ers may feel that doing it this way is not 'real' prayer ministry

But when it is done properly, this combination of oil and anonymity seems to enable many who have never yet found the courage and confidence to respond to God to take this vital first step. Having done it once, and hopefully found it a positive experience, they will much more readily respond again in the future. I remember visiting one church where I asked the vicar whether we might invite people for ministry during the Sunday morning service. He was very hesitant indeed, as nothing like that had ever gone on there before, but I assured him that I knew what I was doing, and that anyway the next week I would be 150 miles away so if it all went pear-shaped he could blame me and promise never to invite me back again. Finally he reluctantly agreed to include ministry, and set up one station for anointing, since he was sure less than half a dozen people would respond. I preached what I remember as a pretty ordinary sermon,

He had been protecting them from prayer ministry because he thought they would not like it

led the 'meditation,' and invited people, if they wanted God to intensify his work in their lives, to receive anointing on their way back from the communion rail. Something over 50 people, from a congregation of about 180, responded, and I ended up closing down the service myself while the vicar still had a huge queue in front of him waiting for anointing. Afterwards he was devastated, 'I've been holding this church back!' he exclaimed in dismay. He had been protecting them from prayer ministry because he thought they would not like it; in fact the response showed they were gagging for it!

The more I have stepped out and offered ministry as I have preached the more I have seen this scenario repeated again and again. People who would never in a million years come forward for more Wimber-style ministry have found that this model allows them to respond in a way which does not hurt a bit! Perhaps the highlight for me was offering prayer ministry at a *Book of Common Prayer* 8 am Holy Communion Service in a highly conservative rural parish church and seeing all but a couple of the congregation receive prayer for the filling of the Holy Spirit one Pentecost Sunday. Anglicans will know that if you can do it there you can do it pretty much anywhere!

6 Just Do It!

I hope you now have enough of a grasp of person-centred prayer ministry to have a go, and perhaps to include it in the life of your church.

Let me say again that it is not a panacea which must replace all other ways of praying for people. You will find that for some purposes and for some people this model just will not work. I have never managed to make it work for raising the dead, for example; I just cannot seem to get past the 'How do you need God to come to you right now?' bit. Similarly some people simply do not do 'pictures,' but can only work through words. If you encounter a situation where you are not getting anywhere, that is all right. Just pray for them in another way. But for many people I have found that person-centred prayer ministry gives them access to the resources of the living God in ways which previously they have never been able to connect with.

The Lord be with you as you have a go!

Notes

1 Although some have questioned his assertion that *every* Christian should be skilled in healing and deliverance. The witness of Acts seems to be that the *Apostles* or other leaders were the ones usually called in to minister.

2 P H Lawrence, *Doing What Comes Supernaturally* (Eastbourne: Kingsway, 1992) p 66f.

3 J Leach, *Developing Prayer Ministry* (Grove Renewal booklet R 1) p 18f.

4 J Leach, *Responding to Preaching* (Grove Worship booklet W 139).

5 For example the one found in the *Common Worship: Pastoral Services* book, p 93.